LITTLE BIG BOOKS

HORSES AND PONIES

DAVID LAMBERT

Editor: Trisha Pike   Designer: Jacky Cowdrey
Picture Researcher: Kathy Brandt

Purnell

1 THE FIRST HORSES

Sixty million years ago there lived a tiny, frightened beast the size of a small dog. It lived in the forests, eating ferns and the soft leaves of trees that grew there. It had four toes on each front foot and three on each back foot. This creature was Eohippus, or dawn horse.

Thirty-five million years ago dawn horse had given rise to Mesohippus, or middle horse. Middle horse was as big as a sheepdog. It had three toes on each foot. But it placed its weight on the big middle toe.

Below: Eohippus was tiny and timid and lived in the prehistoric forests.

Below: The first true horse was Equus, the ancestor of horses.

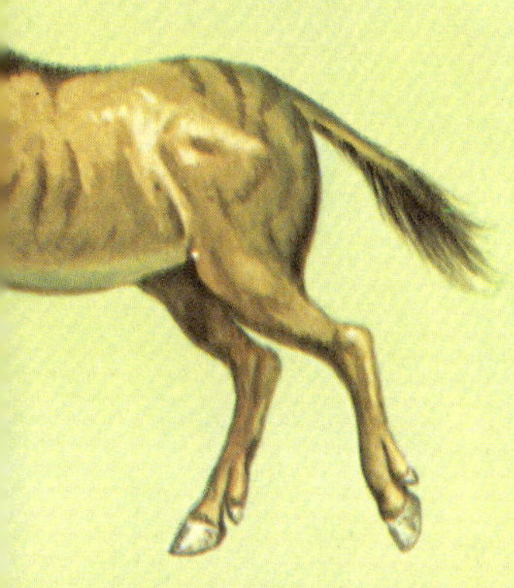

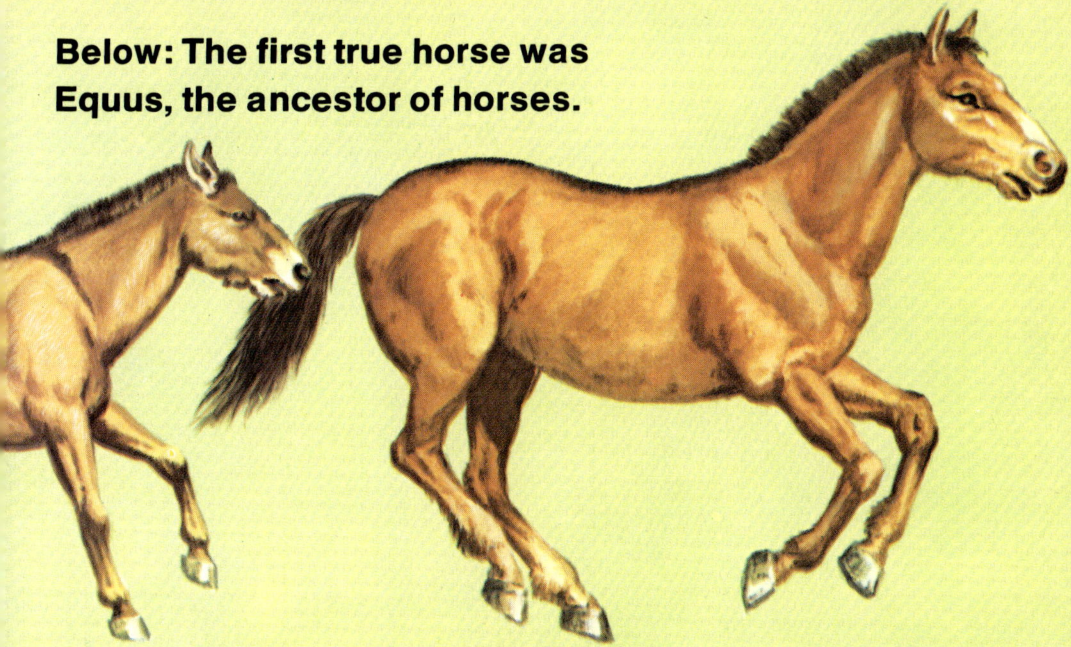

Below: Cud-chewing Merychippus.

Left: Mesohippus ran on tiptoe because in this way it could move very quickly.

By 25 million years ago Merychippus had developed. It lived on the grassy plains instead of the forests, and its teeth had changed so it could grind the grass. Only the middle toe on each of its feet touched the ground and Merychippus could run very swiftly.

Ten million years ago the pony-sized Pliohippus appeared. It was still more like a modern horse. It had lost the other toes on its feet completely. Instead, a hard, horny hoof protected each big middle toe.

Much later Pliohippus evolved into Equus. Equus was the wild ancestor of today's horses.

2 THE HORSE'S BODY

We have seen how the prehistoric
Eohippus gradually changed into
the horse we know today. The front
teeth of the modern horse meet like
pincers, so they nip off blades of
grass easily. Its flat-topped back
teeth grind the grass. Horses also
have a thick, short coat of hair. This
hair helps to stop them getting too
hot or cold.

Horses are always ready for
danger. Their big eyes can see
almost all around. Horses have
short, pointed ears which they can
twitch. This helps them to hear

Left: A horse's body has many parts and each has a special job to do. Its eyes and ears are alert for danger. Its teeth crop grass.

Below: The modern horse survived because it is suited to life on the plains.

sounds coming from any direction.

If danger threatens, a horse can gallop away on its long legs. The back legs give the power for jumping and galloping. The front legs take the shock each time the horse lands. They have big muscles in each upper leg and this gives the power to thrust the leg.

The weight of the body rests on the hooves. That is why they are so large. At the back of each hoof is the frog. This is an elastic pad like a rubber heel. It takes the shock each time the hoof comes down.

Above: A horse's hoof, showing the shoe nails. Right: The V-shaped frog is on the underside.

3   RUNNING WILD

At first, all horses ran wild on the
grassy plains of Asia and America.
These horses were Equus, the first
true horses and the ancestors of
today's horses. Gradually the
American horses died out. But the
Asian horses flourished. They gave
rise to several kinds of wild horses.

One was a small, sturdy, yellow
beast with a short, stiff, black mane.
This horse galloped fast over open
grasslands. Thousands of years ago
Stone Age hunters painted pictures
of it on cave walls. Today, these

early paintings can still be seen in caves in France and Spain.

About 100 years ago a Russian explorer found a few of these horses still living wild. People named this kind of horse Przhevalsky's horse after the explorer who found it. Most Przhevalsky's horses no longer run wild but now live in zoos.

Another type of wild horse lived in the forests of Europe. This was the Tarpan. Wild Tarpans were stocky and probably grayish. Scientists know about them only from the bones they have dug up. But zoos have bred horses very like the wild Tarpans must have been.

4 TAMED FOR WORK

Stone Age hunters killed herds of wild horses for food. Thousands of years passed before people learned to tame them and put them to work.

About 4,000 years ago the people of south west Asia began making horses pull loads. Men joined one end of a pole to a chariot, a kind of two-wheeled cart. They laid the other end of the pole on a saddle resting on a horse's back. People tied that end of the pole to the horse by a girth strap around the horse's belly. The girth strap was joined to a breast strap. When the horse pushed

Below: As the early people settled down and became farmers they tamed wild horses to help them with their work.

against the breast strap it pulled the chariot along.

Later, when horses pulled heavy carts, the breast straps half choked horses. Then people replaced breast straps with padded horse collars. This happened about 700 years ago.

Bareback riding began perhaps 3,000 years ago. But by 1,500 years ago saddles and stirrups had made riding safer. Later still people began to make metal horseshoes to protect the horses' hooves from wear. All these inventions made horses very useful indeed.

Below: Horses of ancient times wore many kinds of metal shoes.

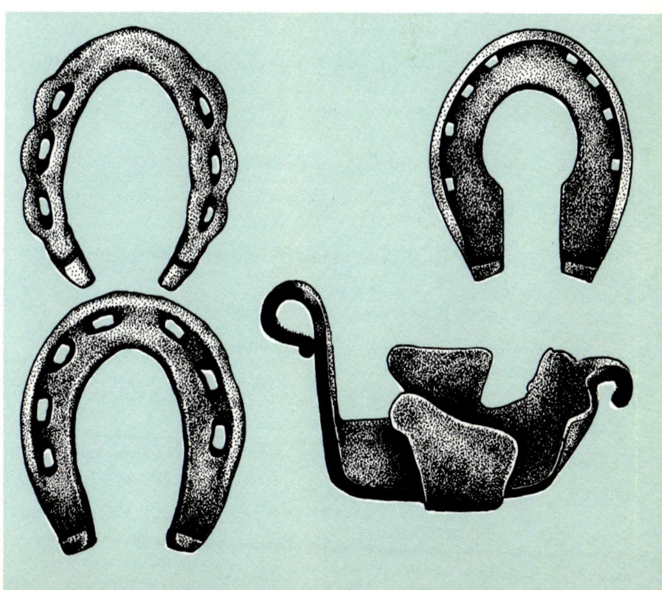

5 HORSES AND PONIES

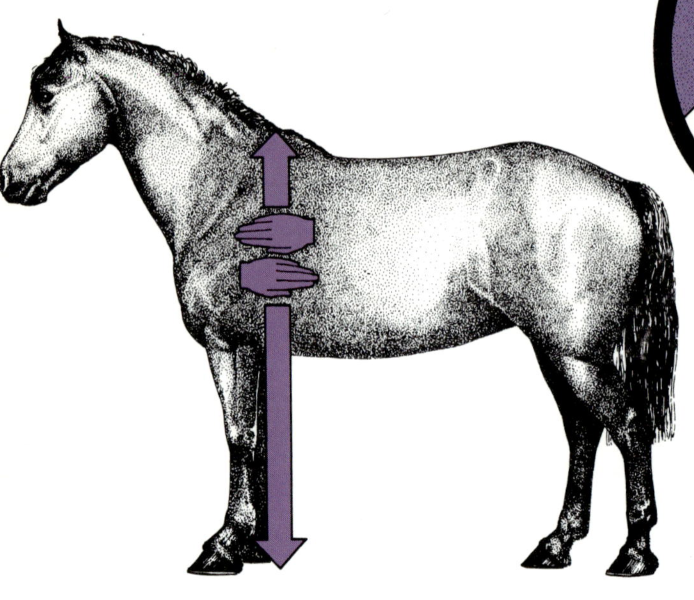

Left: A horse's height is measured at its withers by a hand's depth.

When people began to tame wild horses, most of them were too small for riding or for pulling carts. So people kept only the biggest horses. The foals of these horses often grew bigger than most wild horses. In this way they gradually bred the large modern horse.

Other people bred tiny horses as children's pets. In time there were horses of many sizes. People came to use the word horse for the larger kinds. They called small, full-grown horses ponies.

To tell if a full-grown animal is a

horse or a pony you measure its height at the withers. The withers is the ridge that runs between the shoulder bones.

People measure the height of horses and ponies in hands. At first a hand was the depth of the palm of a man's hand. But some men's hands are larger than others. So people fixed the length of a hand at four inches. Horsemen say that a full-grown horse is over 14 hands 2 inches high, and a pony is under 14 hands 2 inches.

The smallest ponies stand little more than knee-high to a man. But a large horse's withers tower above a tall man's head.

Above: The Palomino. Note the unusual facial colorations.

People often describe horses and ponies by their colors. Some have whole colors—one color almost all over. Blacks are all black. Browns are dark brown or black with light muzzles. Duns are grayish yellow with black manes and tails. Bays are reddish brown with black manes.

Chestnuts are all reddish but come in various shades. Golden chestnuts are often called sorrels. Very pale chestnuts are creams. Palominos are creamy yellow or golden with pale manes and tails.

Below: A skewbald horse grazes contentedly in a grassy field.

Grays are white horses. They are often dappled (covered with cloudy spots). Grays are born nearly black and get pale with age. The only pure white horses are albinos.

Other horses have mixed colors. For instance, piebalds have black and white patches. Skewbalds have patches of white and another color. Appaloosas are white with spots of various colors.

Some horses have special markings. If a horse has white lower legs horsemen say it has stockings or socks. A horse with a big white patch on the face has a blaze.

Above: If a dark horse has a white patch spread over its forehead, the mark is known as a blaze.

Below: A gray can be any shade of white to dark gray.

7 PONIES OF THE WORLD

Above: This Fjord foal will have to work when it is an adult.

There are many different breeds of pony in the world. Some ponies work for their living. Some live in the wild, fending for themselves in forests, mountains and moorlands.

Farmers in the hills of Norway are helped in their work by strong, gentle Fjord ponies. These ponies help to plow the hillside fields. They move easily over steep mountain paths, carrying packs and pulling small carts for their masters. The herdsmen of Mongolia ride tough, strong hill ponies that can survive even severe frost and live on poor food.

Left: Mongolian ponies can withstand bitter weather.

Britain has more native ponies than any country in the world. There are nine kinds of small, hardy ponies living on windy hills in different parts of the British Isles. In fact the world's smallest and sturdiest breed is the Shetland pony, found in Scotland.

Wild ponies are shy. But once they are tamed they make good pets and willing mounts. Young children often learn to ride on Shetland ponies. Older children enjoy pony trekking, when groups ride their ponies for days over the moors.

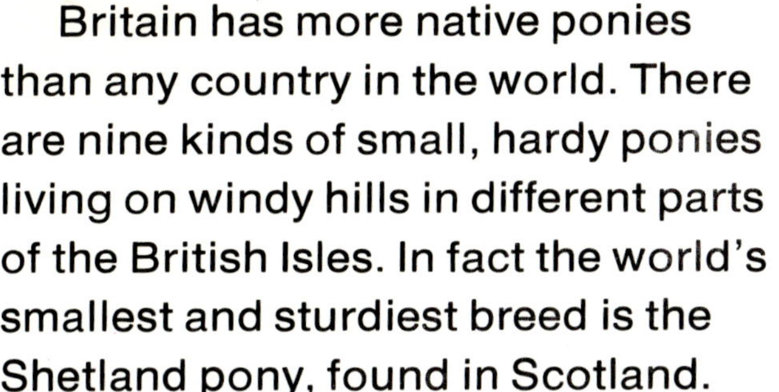

Below: Ponies enjoy trekking as much as their riders for they feel quite at home in the hills.

8   HOME ON THE RANGE

Cowboys look after huge herds of cattle on ranches. This job often means moving far and fast over rough and difficult ground.

At one time, the only way that the cowboy could travel was on horseback. His horse was a cowboy's most precious possession. The creature was small, tough, and wiry.

But first it had to be tamed, for it came from herds of wild horses that once roamed the prairies. These herds in turn came from horses shipped to America by Spanish soldier-explorers about 400 years ago. Many horses escaped and ran

Above: Bucking broncos are ridden at rodeos which are held all over America and Canada.

free. The Indians learned how to catch and ride some of them. Later, the cowboys did so too.

A wild horse would buck, jump, and plunge to throw off its rider. But, once tamed, it would help him round up the cattle for counting. His horse would also carry him day after day as he drove the cattle to market. A good cow horse also knew how to head off a stray and bring it back to the herd.

Today, trains and trucks do much of the work once done by the horse. But cowboys still ride bucking broncos at rodeos.

Left: In the past cowboys went everywhere on horseback.

Above: The Greeks rode into battle against unmounted enemies.

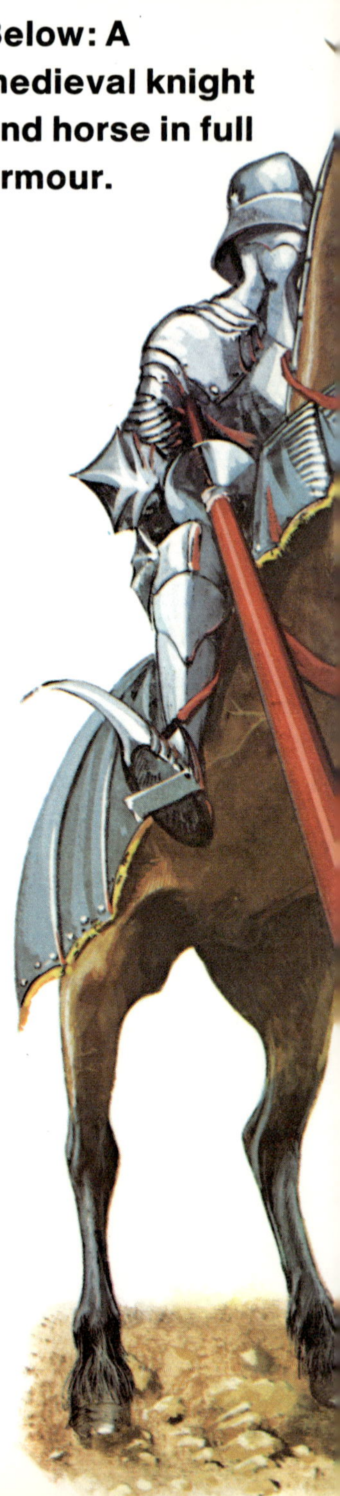

Below: A medieval knight and horse in full armour.

9   AT WAR

All soldiers at first fought on foot. But horses gallop faster than soldiers can run. They are taller than men, too. Soldiers with horses therefore had an advantage in battle.

Early armies did not have horses big enough to be ridden. But later, the Greeks had bigger horses for riding. But they used them only for surprise attacks.

In the Middle Ages people bred very big, strong horses. They were needed to carry knights wearing heavy armor. A knight in full armor

would weigh as much as 210 pounds and his horse would also wear armor.

The invention of guns changed the part played by horses in war. The French general Napoleon used teams of big horses to pull heavy guns into battle. But Hussars, armed only with pistols, rode fast, light, strong horses.

About 100 years ago troops began to use quick-firing guns. Machineguns could easily kill horses and riders. Horses became useless in war and tanks soon took their place.

Below: Teams of horses pulled guns for Napoleon's army.

10 HORSE POWER

At one time, the fastest way to travel was on a galloping horse. In the same way, only horses or oxen could move heavy weights.

In those days horses did all kinds of work. For instance, messengers carried letters on horseback. Businessmen went to work on horseback. Travelers rode in horse-drawn coaches. Even the first buses were pulled by horses.

People used different kinds of horses to do different kinds of jobs.

Below: In days gone by teams of horses pulled the buses.

Above: A 19th-century carriage, whip and lamp.

Below: In Nigeria this tax collector rides to work.

Big, strong farm horses hauled plows and farm carts. High-stepping hackney horses pulled cabs and milk carts. Small ponies worked in coal mines. They hauled coal trucks through low tunnels under the ground. People also used light riding horses to take them everywhere on short journeys. They called such horses hacks.

Then came strong, fast-moving machines. A train or car could travel faster than a horse. A tractor or truck could outpull a team of horses. People needed work horses less than before, and so fewer were bred. Now most kinds of work horses are difficult to find.

11 AT THE RACES

Horses line up at a closed gate. Each carries a small, light rider called a jockey. Suddenly a bell rings and the gate flies open. The jockeys urge their mounts forward. Hooves thunder as the horses pound over the turf. Watching crowds shout. A horse race has begun.

The horses gallop as fast as they can over a long grass track. The first horse past a marked line is the winner. Its owner may receive a big money prize.

Horse races began more than 2,000 years ago. Greeks and Romans raced chariots around

Above: (1.) A jockey has short stirrups so that (2.) he can rise out of the saddle.

Below: These jockeys urge their horses round the course at a gallop.

tracks with sharp bends. Men mounted on horseback were soon racing each other. Modern horse racing began about 300 years ago.

Horses can gallop as fast as most people drive a car today. But some horses are faster than others. The world's fastest horses once came from the deserts of Arabia.

People in Europe bought fast, graceful Arab horses. Then they carefully bred from these. In time the breeders produced an even faster, stronger type. This new breed was the Thoroughbred. Thoroughbreds are today's best racehorses.

Below: The Arab horse once lived with Arabic tribes in the desert.

12 OVER THE JUMPS

Horses can jump high and far. Some can jump as high as a tall man wearing a top hat. Others can clear jumps as long as a bus. Many riders enjoy taking their horses over difficult obstacles.

People race horses over jumps. Such horse races are called steeplechases. Jockeys rode the first steeplechases across country, jumping over whatever obstacles were in their path. They used church steeples to guide them and this is how the race got its name.

Below: Fences set out in a show jumping arena.

Below: This painting shows the first known steeplechase to take place.

Above: This illustration shows how a horse and young rider jump a fence.

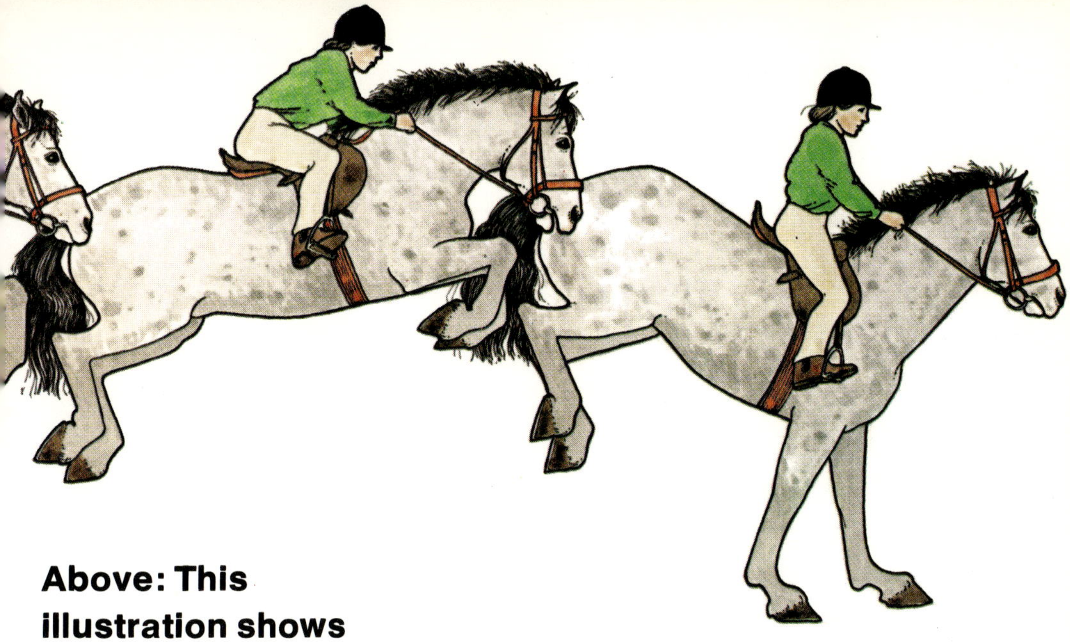

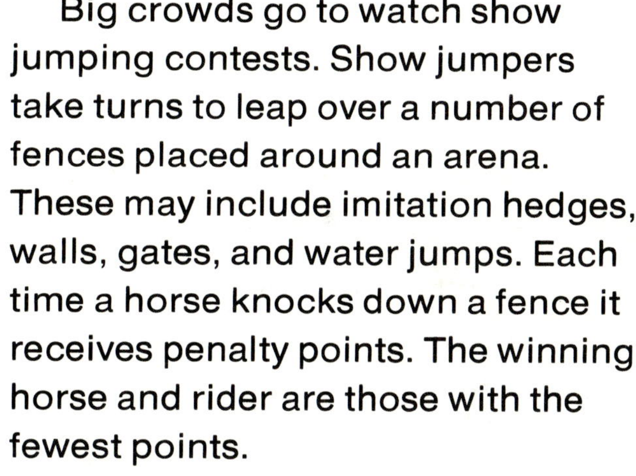

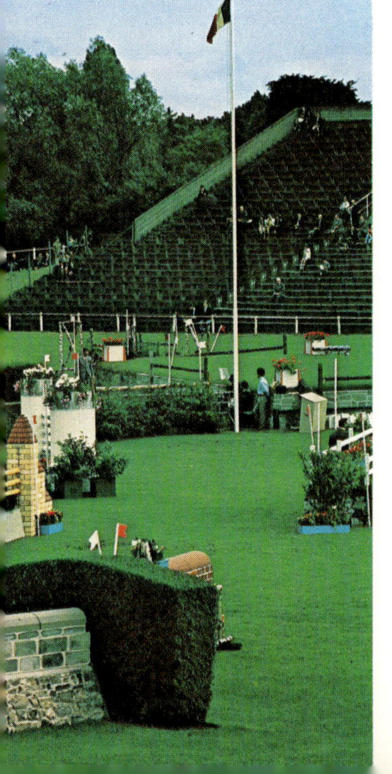

Big crowds go to watch show jumping contests. Show jumpers take turns to leap over a number of fences placed around an arena. These may include imitation hedges, walls, gates, and water jumps. Each time a horse knocks down a fence it receives penalty points. The winning horse and rider are those with the fewest points.

If several horses have the same number of points, they jump again. This time the fences may be raised or the winner may be the horse that goes around in the shortest time. Supple, obedient horses and ponies make the best show jumpers.

13 CIRCUS TIME

A circus horse usually does one of three kinds of work. Some horses are used for bareback riding. The rider is often a girl acrobat. As her horse canters around the ring she may leap on and off. She may even jump from its back, turn a somersault, and land on the back of another horse. Horses for this kind of work must have broad backs. They must also keep up a steady canter around the ring. These horses are called rosinbacks.

A second kind of circus horse

Below: Acrobats balance on the level backs of these rosinbacks.

performs high school acts. High school horses can trot on the spot. They can leap high in the air and kick out all four legs at once. High school horses can even stand and hop on their back legs.

The third kind of circus horse is the liberty horse. Liberty horses have no riders. But they obey a trainer who stands in the circus ring. The trainer tells each horse what to do by calling its name or cracking a whip. The horses move around the ring and form patterns at his command. As many as 16 liberty horses may take part in one act.

Above: It takes two years to train a high school horse to do difficult tricks such as standing on its back legs.

Below: These highly trained liberty horses are from Denmark.

14   A NEW LIFE BEGINS

One day a mare begins to feel
restless. She lies down. Then she
stands. Then she turns in her stable
and paws the ground. She seems to
know that something special is
going to happen.

The mare is right. Soon she lies
down and gives birth to a foal—a
baby horse. Some foals are colts. A
colt is a male foal. But this foal is a
filly—a female foal!

At first the filly lies still. But about
ten minutes later she tries to stand
up. Her legs are long and
spindly—nearly as long as the legs
of a full-grown horse. The filly

**Above: This foal
is only a few
hours old but it
was born with its
eyes open.**

Above: The same foal already can stand and even balance on only three legs.

wobbles and falls. But soon she can walk properly. Within only a few hours she can also run.

For food she drinks milk from her mother's body. After six months she no longer needs milk. She can now feed on grass.

Our young horse grows fast. At one year old she is already half grown. By three years old she may run with a stallion (a male horse). Eleven months later she could give birth to a foal of her own. By five years old our young horse is a full-grown mare like her mother.

Left: For six months after it has been born the young foal will feed on milk from its mother.

15. DONKEYS AND ZEBRAS

The horse has two well known
cousins: the donkey and zebra.

Most donkeys are smaller than
horses and many are gray in color.
There are wild donkeys in hot, dry
parts of Africa and Asia. But most
donkeys are tamed. They are strong
and sure-footed beasts. In some
lands farmers use donkeys to carry
heavy loads along rough tracks.

Donkeys and horses can
interbreed. A donkey father and a
horse mother produce a mule. Mules

Left: This donkey father and horse mother have produced a mule. The young mule will grow to be as big and strong as its horse mother.

Below: A donkey hard at work, carrying water from a well in hot and dusty Tunisia, in North Africa.

are strong and as big as horses. A donkey mother and a horse father produce a hinny. Hinnies are donkey-sized. Mules and hinnies cannot have young of their own.

Zebras are really horses with black and white stripes. No two zebras have the same pattern of stripes. Every zebra has a different pattern on each side.

Zebras live in the hot grasslands of Africa. People have often tried to tame them, but with almost no success. They roam in groups and lions catch and kill many of them. But zebras have some defense. They can run fast and can kick hard.

Below: The stripes of zebras make them hard to see in grassland.

WORDS YOU MAY NOT KNOW

Acrobat   A person trained as a professional gymnast.

Arena   An area set aside for public events, such as sports or open-air theater.

Bred   Animals developed by man so as to produce certain qualities in them such as strength or short, heavy legs.

Broncos   Untamed or half-tamed horses.

Canter   Fast pace between a trot and a full gallop.

Cavalry   Military force made up of mounted troops.

Girth strap   Strap that goes around the middle of the horse and helps to suppport the saddle.

Hussar   A soldier who belongs to a light cavalry regiment, or horse army.

Mane   The long hair on the neck and shoulders of certain animals such as the horse and lion.

Mount   To get up on the back of a horse.

Muzzle   The nose and mouth of an animal.

Penalty   A kind of punishment given out when something is done the wrong way.

Pincers   A tool for grasping or nipping anything.

Pony trekking   A journey made on ponies, usually over wild mountain paths.

Stray   An animal that is separated from the herd.

Turf   The covering of grass and other plants that forms the surface of a grassy track.